DATE DUE		
SEP 2 0 1990	FEB 09 1990	
NOV 8 1990	FEB 2 4 1999	
FEB 1 7 1993	MAR 0 9 1999	
SEP 1 1 1995	MAR 1 6 1999	
JAN 0 2 1996	APR 0 1 1999	
MAR 1 4 1996	JAN 2 0 2001	
MAR 0 1 1997		
DEC 08 1998	FEB 2 8 2001	
DEC 1 7 1998	JAN 2 4 2003	
DEC 2 3 1998		
JAN 28 1999		
FEB 02 1999		

Greenwillow
Read-alone

JUDITH S. SEIXAS

WATER
WHAT IT IS,
WHAT IT DOES

illustrated by TOM HUFFMAN

GREENWILLOW BOOKS · New York

Library of Congress
Cataloging-in-Publication Data
Seixas, Judith S.
Water—what it is, what it does.
(A Greenwillow read-alone book)
Summary: A simple introduction
to water, describing its properties,
uses, and interaction with
people and the environment.
Includes five basic experiments.
1. Water—Juvenile literature.
[1. Water]   I. Title.
II. Huffman, Tom, ill.
III. Series: Greenwillow
read-alone books.
GB662.3.S44   1987
553.7   86-14926
ISBN 0-688-06607-0
ISBN 0-688-06608-9 (lib. bdg.)

The preseparated art was
printed in two colors.
The text typeface is Primer.

Text copyright © 1987 by Judith S. Seixas
Illustrations copyright © 1987 by Tom Huffman

First Edition

10 9 8 7 6 5 4 3 2 1

For Eli—with love

from his grandma

—J. S. S.

Love and joy for A. J.

—T. H.

CONTENTS

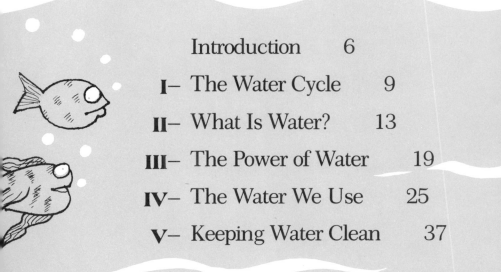

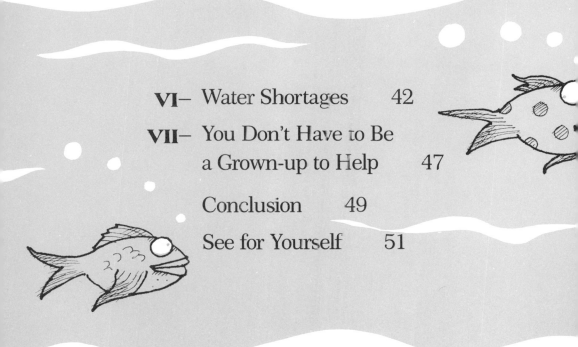

SINCE THE
BEGINNING OF TIME

INTRODUCTION

The water in our sinks today

has been on Earth

for billions of years.

All the water we have

has been on our planet

since the beginning of time.

BEFORE US?

It filled our lakes,

rivers, and oceans

long before

the age of dinosaurs.

There is no new water.

The same large water supply

has been used over

and over again.

But there are more and more
people on Earth
than ever before.

Farms and industries
use more and more water.

We need more clean water every day.
Water is as necessary to us
as the air we breathe.

1

THE WATER CYCLE

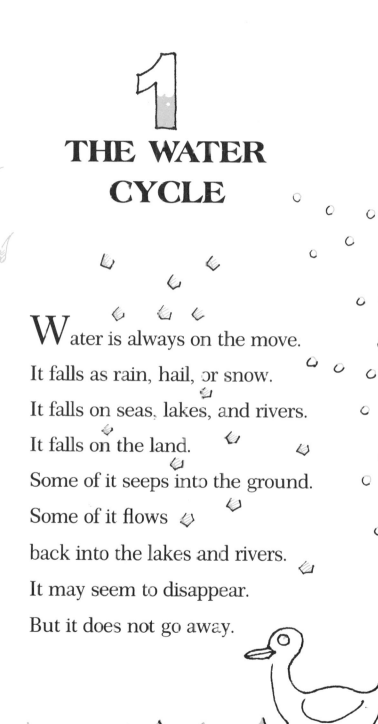

Water is always on the move.

It falls as rain, hail, or snow.

It falls on seas, lakes, and rivers.

It falls on the land.

Some of it seeps into the ground.

Some of it flows

back into the lakes and rivers.

It may seem to disappear.

But it does not go away.

Evaporation

As the sun warms the earth,

water rises into the air

as water vapor.

This is called evaporation.

Water evaporates from oceans, lakes,

plants, animals, and people.

As water vapor rises, it cools

and forms tiny water droplets.

Together droplets form clouds.

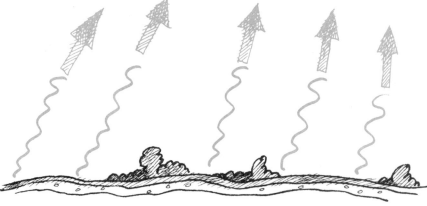

Clouds move wherever
the winds blow them.
When clouds become cool
and heavy with water,
drops fall to earth as rain.

When the air is cold enough,
drops fall as hail or snow.

In time,
all water
becomes part
of this cycle.

People and the Water Cycle

Human beings also play a part
in the water cycle.
Nearly three-fourths of our bodies
consist of water.
All water that enters and
leaves our bodies
becomes part of the cycle.
We take in about two quarts of water
a day by eating and drinking.
When we urinate, urine finally goes
into the ground or waterways.
When we perspire, water evaporates
back into the air.

WHAT IS
WATER?

Water is made up of
hydrogen and oxygen.
Two atoms of hydrogen combine
with one atom of oxygen
to form a molecule of water.
Scientists write it: H_2O

There are billions of water molecules
in a single drop of water.

Gas, Liquid, Solid

Water has three forms:
gas, liquid, and solid.
At room temperature
water is a *liquid*
When it is heated
to a high temperature
(100° Celsius/212° Fahrenheit)
it becomes a gas.
The gas form of water
is called *steam*.
When water is cooled enough
(below 0° Celsius /32° Fahrenheit)
it becomes a solid.
The solid form of water
is called *ice*.

Pure water has no color.

But most water is not pure.

It has particles

and tiny gas bubbles in it.

Most of them we cannot see.

In light, these particles

reflect the colors that

surround the water.

When water is under the blue sky,

it looks blue.

When water is in a green bowl,

it looks green.

When there is no light,

there is no reflection.

So at night a lake looks black.

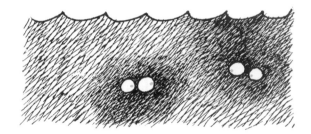

When particles in water

are large enough to see,

water takes on the color

of the particles.

For example,
water with soil
in it looks brown.

Water takes on the shape
of the space it is in.
In a pond it is the shape
of the pond.

In a pail it is the shape of the pail.

Water Is Tasteless

Pure water has no taste or smell.

When water has a taste or smell,

it has impurities in it.

These impurities come from the pipes

through which the water runs.

They come from minerals in the ground.

Or they come from particles in the air

through which rain falls.

3

THE POWER
OF WATER

Have you ever poured water on sand?
The water seeps into the sand.
It moves between the grains.
Flowing water moves
loose soil and stones.
It changes the shape
of the land.

Water changes the shape of beaches.

It cuts ruts and paths.

It cuts away cliffs.

It deepens river banks.

The Grand Canyon was formed as the Colorado River cut into the earth.

Water also pushes and rolls
rocks against each other.
In time, rough rocks are ground
into smooth pebbles and sand.
The power of water never stops
changing the shape of the land.

W ater can also do damage.

Movement of sand or soil by water

is called erosion.

Heavy rain can cause rivers

to flood and deeply erode soil.

Rain washes soil into rivers.

Rivers wash soil and sand

into lakes and seas.

Good soil is washed away

from farm lands.

Without soil, crops cannot be grown.

One way we can prevent erosion
is by keeping the land planted.
Roots hold soil in place.
We keep roots in the ground by:

✓ saving trees.

✓ farming, or growing
  backyard gardens.

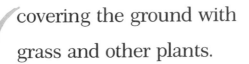

✓ covering the ground with
  grass and other plants.

✓ growing bushes and plants
  on river banks.

✓ keeping sand dunes covered
  with beach grass.

Scientists have learned
how to use falling water
to make electricity.
They channel water to fall
so that it will turn a wheel,
or turbine.

Turbines are placed below dams
or at the bottom of waterfalls.
The turbine turns a generator,
which makes electricity.
In this way water power
is turned into electrical power.
Electrical power
made from water power
is known as hydroelectric power.

4
THE WATER
WE USE

Earth is the only planet
with large amounts of water.
But nearly all our water (97%)
is in the salty seas.
Salt water cannot be used for
drinking, washing, or cooking.
It cannot be used for farming.
It cannot be given to animals.

Surface Water

Our remaining water (3%) is fresh.

But three-fourths of it is frozen

in ice caps at the North and South Poles.

Therefore, only
a very small part
(less than 1%)
of the water on Earth
can be used
for our daily needs.

A large part of our usable water
is beneath the Earth's surface.
Groundwater is found between
grains of sand, gravel, and soil.
Some is in porous rock.
A porous rock is like a hard sponge.
It is full of holes.
Groundwater seeps into
all the unfilled spaces.

POROUS ROCK ➡

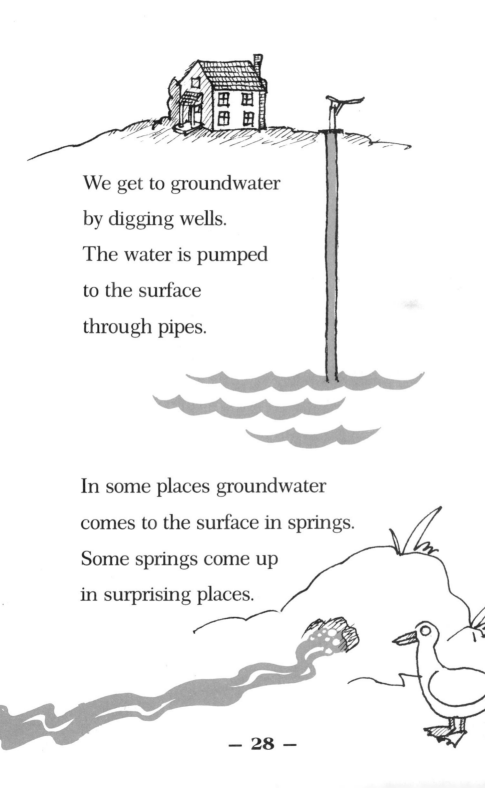

We get to groundwater
by digging wells.
The water is pumped
to the surface
through pipes.

In some places groundwater
comes to the surface in springs.
Some springs come up
in surprising places.

Have you ever gone swimming
in a lake?
You can feel cold spots.
This cold water comes
from springs at
the bottom
of the lake.

Because spring water runs into rivers,
many rivers are full
even when it has not rained.

SURE IS FULL TODAY!

Aquifers

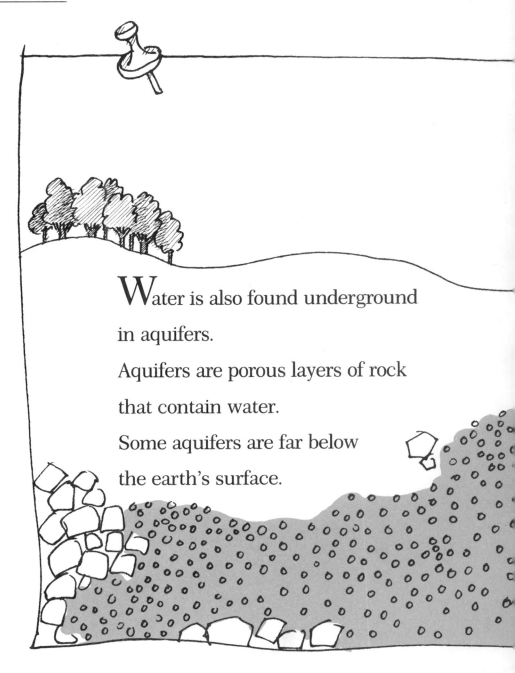

Water is also found underground in aquifers.

Aquifers are porous layers of rock that contain water.

Some aquifers are far below the earth's surface.

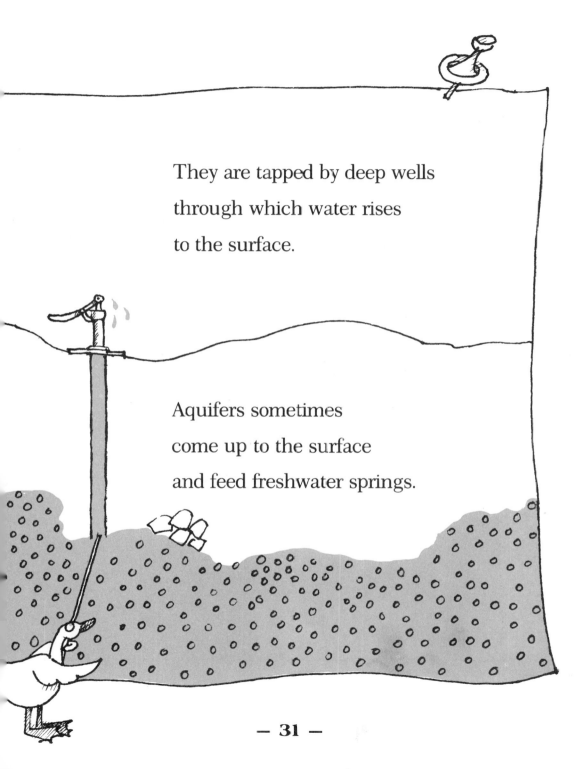

They are tapped by deep wells
through which water rises
to the surface.

Aquifers sometimes
come up to the surface
and feed freshwater springs.

The Water Table

The highest level
that underground water reaches
is called the water table.
In rainy times the water
seeps down into the earth.
The water table rises.

In dry spells,

when the water

flows away

or evaporates,

the water table drops.

It also drops when

water is pumped

out of the ground.

Man-made Water Storage

Man has had to learn
to store water.
Much of the water
we use daily
is stored in man-made lakes
called reservoirs.

Reservoirs are made by building dams to keep water from flowing away. The water is collected from rivers and streams.

Rain and melting snow increase the amount of water in reservoirs.

In some parts of the world,
rainwater used for drinking
and washing is stored in
above-ground tanks
or in underground tanks
called cisterns.
They are filled by rain
collected from the rooftops.
The water is piped down
from roofs into the tanks
or cisterns.

Tanks and cisterns are used
mainly in dry areas where only
a small amount of rain falls.

5

KEEPING
WATER
CLEAN

How is it that water

that has been used over and over

for millions of years

is still fit to drink?

Today we have man-made filters

to clean up our water,

and we have laws to help *keep* it clean.

Water is purified naturally when:

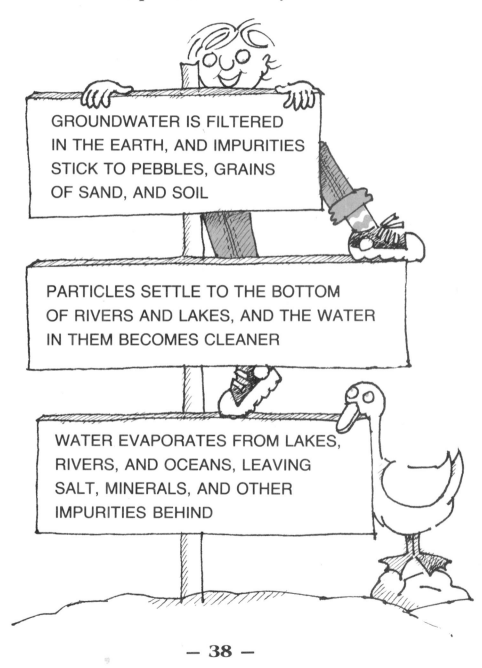

GROUNDWATER IS FILTERED IN THE EARTH, AND IMPURITIES STICK TO PEBBLES, GRAINS OF SAND, AND SOIL

PARTICLES SETTLE TO THE BOTTOM OF RIVERS AND LAKES, AND THE WATER IN THEM BECOMES CLEANER

WATER EVAPORATES FROM LAKES, RIVERS, AND OCEANS, LEAVING SALT, MINERALS, AND OTHER IMPURITIES BEHIND

Much of our surface water
and groundwater is being polluted
with harmful chemicals and germs.
This water cannot be used
for drinking.
It can be poisonous.

Water becomes polluted when:

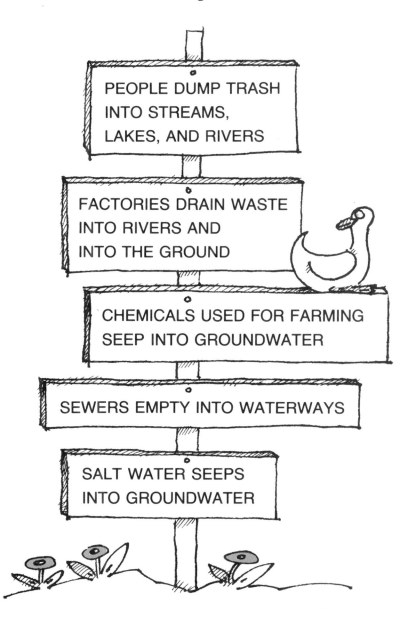

PEOPLE DUMP TRASH INTO STREAMS, LAKES, AND RIVERS

FACTORIES DRAIN WASTE INTO RIVERS AND INTO THE GROUND

CHEMICALS USED FOR FARMING SEEP INTO GROUNDWATER

SEWERS EMPTY INTO WATERWAYS

SALT WATER SEEPS INTO GROUNDWATER

Water also gathers impurities
when it falls as rain.
If the air is impure,
particles are picked up
in every drop.
Air kept free of smoke and fumes
will help keep our rainwater pure.

If we pollute water faster
than it is purified,
the day may come when
there will not be enough water for
people, animals, and farming.

6

WATER SHORTAGES

The people on Earth use billions of gallons of water each day. Most of it is used by industry. A small part is used for drinking, cooking, bathing, laundering, and flushing.

When we use water faster

than it can be replaced

we create a *water shortage.*

When there is less rainfall

than is usual,

water shortages occur.

When reservoirs and cisterns dry up,

the *water table goes down.*
In cities the pavement

keeps rainwater from seeping

into the ground.

Water for cities must be piped
from distant reservoirs.

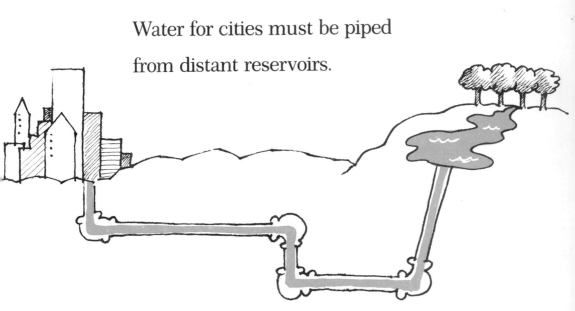

Or it must be pumped
from nearby rivers and then purified.

No matter where you live,
city or country,
there must be a supply
of fresh water.

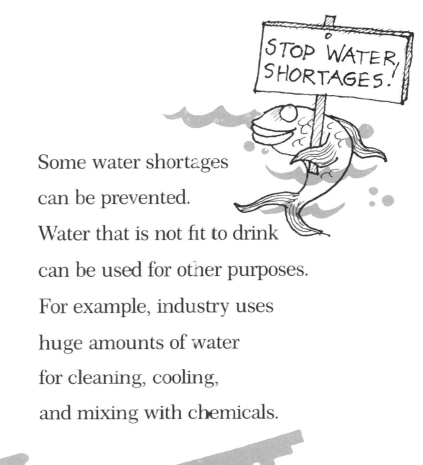

Some water shortages
can be prevented.
Water that is not fit to drink
can be used for other purposes.
For example, industry uses
huge amounts of water
for cleaning, cooling,
and mixing with chemicals.

When factories are careful,
the same water can be used
again and again.

Water used to wash cars does not have to be pure. Car washes can use the same water more than once.

Plants can live with water that is not pure.

In some places sinks and tubs can drain into gardens.

Much of the water we use daily can and should be used more than once.

YOU DON'T HAVE TO BE A GROWN-UP TO HELP

Here is how you can help

cut down on water use:

✓ Use less water for your bath.

✓ Turn off taps when you are not using them.

✓ Don't run water while you brush your teeth.

✓ If you don't drink
all the water in your glass,
pour what is left on a plant.

✓ Report leaky pipes and faucets.

✓ Flush the toilet
only when you have to.

✓ Don't tramp on grass.
The roots hold water in the soil.

✓ Collect rainwater
for plants and animals.

These may seem like small savings,
but every drop counts.

CONCLUSION

All people, animals, and plants
need water to live.
We can live for a few weeks
without food.
But we can live only a few days
without water.
Now you know how important
our water is.
You know how it is used and misused.
As time goes on we will need
more drinking water.
We will need more water
for farming.

Scientists have tried for years

to discover a cheap way to produce

fresh water from sea water

and polluted water.

But, as yet, the methods

that have been developed

cost too much.

So we must care for the water we have.

An Earth without clean water

would be an Earth without life.

SEE FOR YOURSELF

Experiments

1. SALT AND WATER EVAPORATION

Stir a pinch of salt

into a teaspoonful of water.

Place the water-filled spoon on a plate.

Let it stand for two days.

The water will evaporate.

Where is the salt?

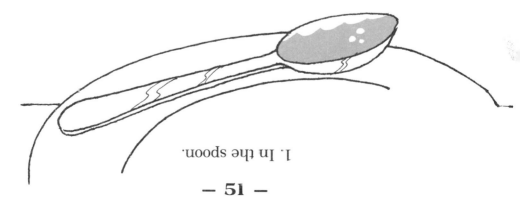

1. In the spoon.

2. EVAPORATION

Take two jars.

Fill them to the same level

with water.

Cover one.

Leave the other open.

Let them stand for two days.

Which one has

more water in it?

2. The covered jar.

3. GROUNDWATER

Fill a glass with sand.

Pour water into the glass.

Where did the water go?

3. Between the grains of sand.

4. EVAPORATION AND HEAT

Put a spoonful of water in a cup.

Put the cup in a warm place.

Put another spoonful of water
in another cup.

Place the cup in a cool spot.

From which cup
does the water
evaporate first?

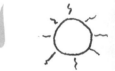

5. PURIFYING WATER

Put some soil into a jar of water.

Cover and shake the jar.

The water becomes muddy.

Let the jar stand for

two days.

What happens to the water?

What happens to the soil?

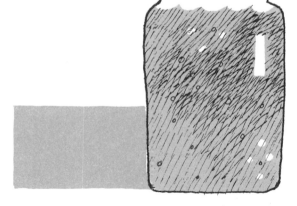

The soil has settled at the bottom of the jar.

5. The water becomes clear.

JUDITH S. SEIXAS was graduated from Carleton College and has an M.A. from Columbia's Teachers College. She has long been involved in health issues, specializing in the treatment of alcoholics and their families. Her wide experience encompasses both the educational and the therapeutic. She is the co-author of *Children of Alcoholism: A Survivor's Manual* and for children the author of: *Drugs—What They Are, What They Do; Vitamins—What They Are, What They Do; Junk Food—What It Is, What It Does; Alcohol—What It Is, What It Does; Tobacco—What It Is, What It Does;* and *Living with a Parent Who Drinks too Much.*

TOM HUFFMAN attended the School of Visual Arts in New York City and holds a B.A. from the University of Kentucky. Mr. Huffman is a free-lance artist whose works have appeared in galleries, advertisements, and national magazines. He has illustrated many children's books, including eight Greenwillow Read-alone Books.